Grades 5–8

Music Makes the Scene

The impact of music on the movies...and on you!

Cathy Blair

Editor: Kris Kropff
Cover and Book Design: Patti Jeffers

© 2008 Heritage Music Press, a division of The Lorenz Corporation, and its licensors. All rights reserved.

Permission to photocopy the student pages in this book is hereby granted to one teacher as part of the purchase price. This permission may only be used to provide copies for this teacher's specific classroom or educational setting. This permission may not be transferred, sold, or given to any additional or subsequent user of this product. Thank you for respecting the copyright laws.

Heritage Music Press
A division of The Lorenz Corporation
P.O. Box 802
Dayton, Ohio 45401
www.lorenz.com

Printed in the United States of America

ISBN: 978-1-4291-0048-9

HERITAGE MUSIC PRESS
Diverse Resources for *Your* Music Classroom
a Lorenz company • www.lorenz.com

Foreword

The 50-minute DVD that is the centerpiece of *Music Makes the Scene* includes ten short (30–45 second) original movie clips. Each is shown once without audio, then three more times, each with different music. Students watch and listen to all four versions of the clip while completing guided-listening activities that highlight how each of the different soundtracks affects the reactions to the movie clip. Reproducible worksheets and listening guides are included in this unique product that brings critical listening alive in your classroom. (The DVD works with any standard DVD player or computer equipped with DVD software.)

—*Kris Kropff, Editor*

Contents

Using *Music Makes the Scene*		3
Film Clip Overview		5

Reproducible Worksheets	Multiple Choice	Writing Intensive
Ancient Egypt	8	9
Crystal Effects	11	12
Do You Like to Fly?	13	14
From the Treetops	16	17
Night Vision	19	20
Mad Rush	21	22
March of the Penguins	23	24
Ocean's Island	26	27
Tales of the Tribesmen	28	29
Episode in Space	31	32

Their Music Makes the Scene (Short biographies of several film composers)	33
Whose Music Made the Scene? (Film-composer quiz)	37
Answer Keys	38

Using *Music Makes the Scene*

Each of the ten professionally filmed clips used on the DVD is presented four times. The first is shown without music. The other three incorporate vastly different styles of music to demonstrate the impact that music has on the movies.

Begin by showing the no-music version of one of the ten film clips. Then, depending on the age and skill level of your class, either discuss the clip—mood, scenery, action, location, etc.—or have your students write their impressions. Several of the reproducible writing-intensive worksheets include "for discussion" questions that could be answered on the reverse side of the worksheet.

Next, show the first example of the clip that includes music. Again, discuss the clip, focusing on how the music affected the movie clip. Did it make it funny, scary, dramatic, romantic, cute, suspenseful? What were the students' perceptions of the clip as compared to the no-music version they viewed first? If your students have the necessary previous experiences, discuss instrumentation, dynamics, texture, style, rhythmic activity, etc. You may also use the worksheets (particularly the multiple-choice examples) to further this exploration.

Repeat this same process for the other two examples with music. After viewing and listening to all four versions of the clip, have the class decide which music made the most sense or seemed to fit the film clip the best. Remind them that there are really no right or wrong answers!

The film clips range in duration from 30 to 45 seconds each. We hope that you will be able to view and evaluate at least two of the ten sequences during a regular class period. Be sure to allow enough time for students to complete the worksheets and discuss their opinions—it is amazing how animated students become when voicing their opinions about which music best fit the clip and why!

Another way to use *Music Makes the Scene* is to have students listen to the music without seeing the video. Have them describe what kind of scene the music evokes; then, compare the images to the film clip.

Reproducible Worksheets

Music Makes the Scene includes two worksheets for each of the ten film-clip groups. One requires solid knowledge of tempo and dynamic terminology, and the ability to identify instruments by sound. It also requires a lot of creative thinking from your students. The other worksheet is a series of multiple-choice questions, so it is a little easier and will take less time to complete. To complete the worksheets, your students will need to hear each music example several times.

These worksheets may be used as a way to help students organize their analysis of each of the music selections associated with a film clip, or students may turn in the worksheets. Add these completed worksheets to students' portfolios or keep them with their grades to help track students' progress in the comprehension of music concepts.

Using the DVD

The DVD will play in any standard DVD player and may also be played using a computer loaded with the software necessary to read a DVD. Use the remote just as you would on any standard DVD to scroll through the different film groups. The arrows on each screen move you between menu pages. Highlight a title and press enter to view a particular example of the clip.

National Standards for Music Education and *Music Makes the Scene*

This unique book and DVD package focuses on the following *National Standards for Music Education* for Grades 5–8:

6. Listening to, analyzing, and describing music.
7. Evaluating music and music performances.
8. Understanding relationships between music, the other arts, and disciplines outside the arts.
9. Understanding music in relation to history and culture.[1]

More specifically, the films and worksheets will help students learn to:

- Describe specific music events (e.g., a solo instrument enters in measure 4, the tempo changes). (6a)
- Analyze the uses of elements of music in aural examples taken from a variety of styles and genres (e.g., the driving eighth-note rhythm of the bass and guitar help build the intensity of the action in the movie). (6b)
- Demonstrate knowledge of the basic principles of meter and rhythm. (6c)
- Develop ways to evaluate effectiveness of a performance and how it relates to other arts. (7a)
- Compare the way music and film interact to seemingly transform events and scenes. (8a)
- Describe distinguishing characteristics of music genres. (9a)
- Compare the roles music serves in movies versus the role it plays in a concert setting. (9c)

Creative Writing and *Music Makes the Scene*

As many music teachers are well aware, virtually every state has its own content standards for English Language Arts in elementary, middle and high school. In one form or another, the various state standards all include a section on written communication skills that emphasizes that these skills are central to learning.

Over the last several years, there has been an emphasis on writing in classes outside of Language Arts. *Music Makes the Scene* and the accompanying worksheets are one of the easiest ways for music teachers to incorporate writing in their classes. Using graphic organizers like Venn diagrams, hierarchy charts and radial diagrams allows students to create a central theme and add words and phrases that relate in specific ways to the theme. These ancillary sections eventually become the sentences and paragraphs that make up a complete composition. If time allows, or in partnership with your students' language-art teachers, these worksheets could be expanded into extended writing assignments.

---

[1] From *National Standards for Arts Education.* Copyright © 1994 by Music Educators National Conference (MENC). Used by permission. The complete National Arts Standards and additional materials relating to the Standards are available from MENC: The National Association for Music Education, 1806 Robert Fulton Drive, Reston, VA 20191; www.menc.org.

Film Clip Overview

The basic instrumentation and tempo of each clip follows. In addition, descriptive words and phrases are listed to give you a general sense of the thoughts behind the music that accompanies each film clip. Of course, you and your students will come up with different descriptions, and that is great too!

Ancient Egypt

Ancient Egypt 1
- Orchestra (strings and woodwinds)
- Sentimental, sad
- Slow, smooth, legato
- Crescendo and decrescendo in each two-measure phrase

Ancient Egypt 2
- Orchestra (strings, brass, percussion)
- Crescendo from beginning to end
- Driving
- Suspenseful

Ancient Egypt 3
- Pop/rock band
- Features organ
- Forceful
- Action-adventure
- "Spy" music

Crystal Effects

Crystal Effects 1
- Solo harpsichord
- Stately, moderately slow
- Wistful
- Processional

Crystal Effects 2
- Orchestra with pop/rock rhythm section
- Vocal effects
- Desperation
- Out of control
- Crazy

Crystal Effects 3
- Brass with pop/rock rhythm section
- Uplifting
- Olympian
- Sports theme

Do You Like to Fly?

Do You Like to Fly? 1
- Orchestra
- Dark
- Scary, foreboding
- Dynamic contrasts
- Decrescendo to end

Do You Like to Fly? 2
- Salsa band
- Happy, carefree
- Fun trip
- Looking forward to a good time

Do You Like to Fly? 3
- World instruments
- No tempo
- Aliens, "other worldly"
- Far out, spacey
- Creepy

From the Treetops

From the Treetops 1
- Rock and roll band
- Wild and crazy
- Party, fun
- Rollicking

From the Treetops 2
- Synthesizer effects/piano
- Floating tempo
- Ethereal
- "Native" undertone
- Danger looming

From the Treetops 3
- Winds and percussion
- "Cartoon" music
- Clowns
- Circus atmosphere
- Fun and zany

Night Vision

Night Vision 1
- Fusion band
- Contemporary, "hip"
- Funky
- Freewheeling
- Solo instrument enters mid-way through

Night Vision 2
- Hard rock
- Edgy, gritty
- "Bad part of town"
- Nasty

Night Vision 3
- Fusion band and synthesizer effects
- Out of tempo
- Voice effects—eerie feeling
- Danger ahead
- Spacey

Mad Rush

Mad Rush 1
- String orchestra
- Mozart, Classical
- Controlled chaos
- Busy, happy city people

Mad Rush 2
- Tenor saxophone and violin with rhythm section
- Light, happy
- Comedy show theme song
- Meeting friends
- "After work"
- Carefree

Mad Rush 3
- Synthesizer and vocal effects
- Out of tempo
- Threatening, menacing
- Alien invasion
- Fear

March of the Penguins

March of the Penguins 1
- Synthesizer and world percussion instruments
- Native sound of natural habitat
- "Documentary" style music
- Dark, exotic

March of the Penguins 2
- Concert band
- Fun and zany
- Wacky, funny
- "Cartoon" music
- Crazy

March of the Penguins 3
- Orchestra and synthesizer effects
- Scary
- Foreboding
- Tension, worry, fear
- Forceful
- "Penguins take over the world"

Ocean's Island

Ocean's Island 1
- Percussion and synthesizer effects
- Mysterious
- Searching
- Uncertainty
- Tension

Ocean's Island 2
- Pop/rock rhythm section
- Driving, forceful
- Frantic
- Adventure

Ocean's Island 3
- Tenor saxophone solo with jazz rhythm section
- Melancholy
- Calm
- Floating
- Serene

Tales of the Tribesmen

Tales of the Tribesmen 1
- World instruments
- Transformation
- Shifting texture
- Transitions

Tales of the Tribesmen 2
- Pop/rock rhythm section
- Two sections that match the two sections of the movie clip:
    - Section 1 is light and transparent; Electric piano is the main instrument
    - Section 2 is dark and thick; Driving rhythms; Electric guitar is the main instrument

Tales of the Tribesmen 3
- Pop/rock rhythm section with vocalese
- Also in two sections:
    - Section 1 is shadowy; the vocal effects evoke feelings of yearning
    - Section 2 is uplifting and hopeful; lots of guitar

Episode in Space

Episode in Space 1
- Synthesizer effects
- Danger looming
- Out of tempo
- Spacey
- Warning
- Crisis approaching

Episode in Space 2
- World effects
- Haunting
- No tempo
- Trouble ahead

Episode in Space 3
- Chamber orchestra
- "Classical"
- Heavenly
- Calming
- Don't worry about outcome, natural occurrence

Name _____

Date _____

Ancient Egypt

As you watch and listen to the three versions of *Ancient Egypt*, circle the letter of the word or group of words that best completes the following statements.

Example 1

1. The two instrument families you hear in this example are _____.
    A. brass and woodwind   B. brass and percussion   C. string and woodwind

2. The tempo of this example could be described as _____.
    A. adagio   B. allegro   C. crescendo

3. _____ best describe the dynamic levels of this example.
    A. *Piano* and *pianissimo*   B. *Forte* and *rallentando*   C. *Crescendo* and *decrescendo*

Example 2

1. _____ is an instrument family not heard in this example.
    A. Brass   B. Woodwind   C. String

2. The term _____ best describes the tempo of this example.
    A. largo   B. allegro   C. sostenuto

3. This example begins *piano* and _____ to the end.
    A. ritards   B. crescendos   C. diminuendos

Example 3

1. The two instrument families heard in this example are _____.
    A. string and brass   B. woodwind and percussion   C. electronic and percussion

2. What is the time signature of this example?
    A. $\frac{3}{4}$ B. $\frac{6}{8}$ C. $\frac{4}{4}$

3. Which term best describes the style of this example?
    A. Classical   B. Blues   C. Rock

From *Music Makes the Scene* by Cathy Blair

Name _____

Date _____

Ancient Egypt

For discussion: What kind of music do you think would be best suited to accompany the short film clip you just watched? Should it be fast or slow? Loud or soft? Would you use electric or acoustic instruments? Would the style of music stay the same throughout? What other musical things can you think of that would help bring this video to life?

As you watch each of the three film clips with music, list three instruments you hear in each example in the boxes below. The first one has been done for you.

Example 1

| Violin | Clarinet | Oboe |

Example 2

| | | |

Example 3

| | | |

From *Music Makes the Scene* by Cathy Blair

Name _____

Date _____

Ancient Egypt (page 2)

As you watch and listen to the clips again, write three words that describe the music with each clip (loud, soft, *staccato, allegro, adagio,* etc.) in the boxes below. Three words that describe the first example are listed for you. Of course, there are many more to choose from!

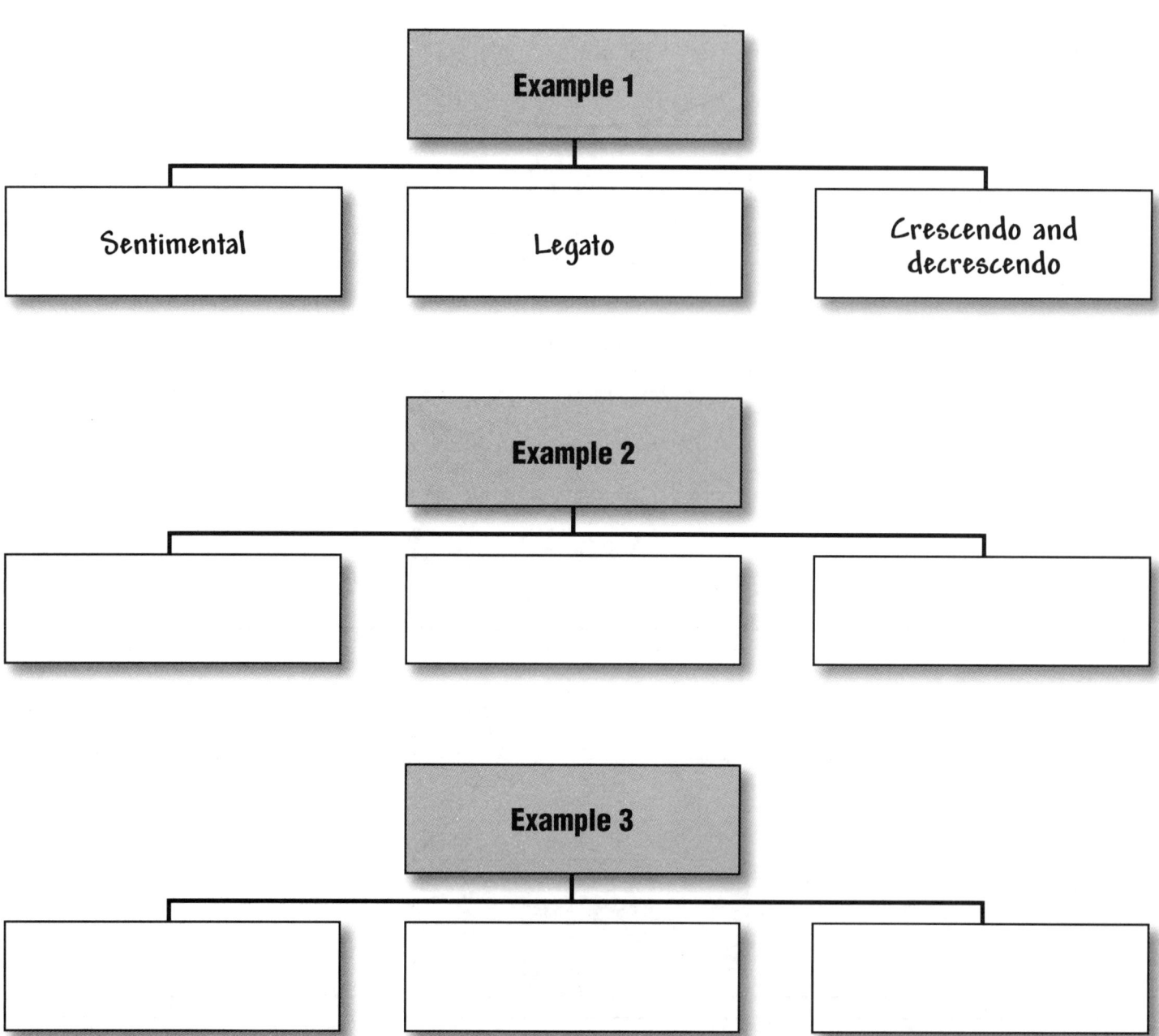

From *Music Makes the Scene* by Cathy Blair

Name _____

Date _____

Crystal Effects

As you watch and listen to the three versions of *Crystal Effects*, circle the letter of the word that best completes the following statements.

Example 1

1. This example is a _____.
   A. duet   B. solo   C. sonata

2. The term _____ best describes the style of this piece.
   A. stately   B. modern   C. brassy

3. _____ is a likely composer of this example.
   A. Johannes Brahms   B. Peter Tchaikovsky C. J.S. Bach

Example 2

1. The first section of this example uses _____-measure phrases.
   A. 6   B. 3   C. 4

2. What is the time signature of this example?
   A. $\frac{6}{8}$ B. $\frac{12}{8}$ C. $\frac{4}{4}$

3. How would you describe the bass part of the first section of this example?
   A. Descending   B. Ascending   C. Stationary

Example 3

1. _____ is one of the instrument families heard in this example.
   A. Brass   B. Woodwind   C. String

2. You might expect to hear this style of music in a movie about _____.
   A. animals   B. sports   C. love

3. The _____ play the melody most of the time in this example.
   A. trumpets   B. violins   C. woodwinds

From *Music Makes the Scene* by Cathy Blair

Name _____

Date _____

Crystal Effects

For discussion: What kind of music do you think would be best suited to accompany the short film clip you just watched? Should it be fast or slow? Loud or soft? Would it feature electric or acoustic instruments? Would the style of music stay the same throughout? What other musical things can you think of that would help bring this movie to life?

As you watch each of the three film clips with music, fill out the charts below. In the left-most box of each chart, write a word or phrase that describes the tempo of the music that accompanies the scene. In the middle box, list one of the instruments you hear in the clip. In the right-most box, describe any dynamic changes that occur in the clip (all *piano*; begins *forte*, ends *piano*; etc.).

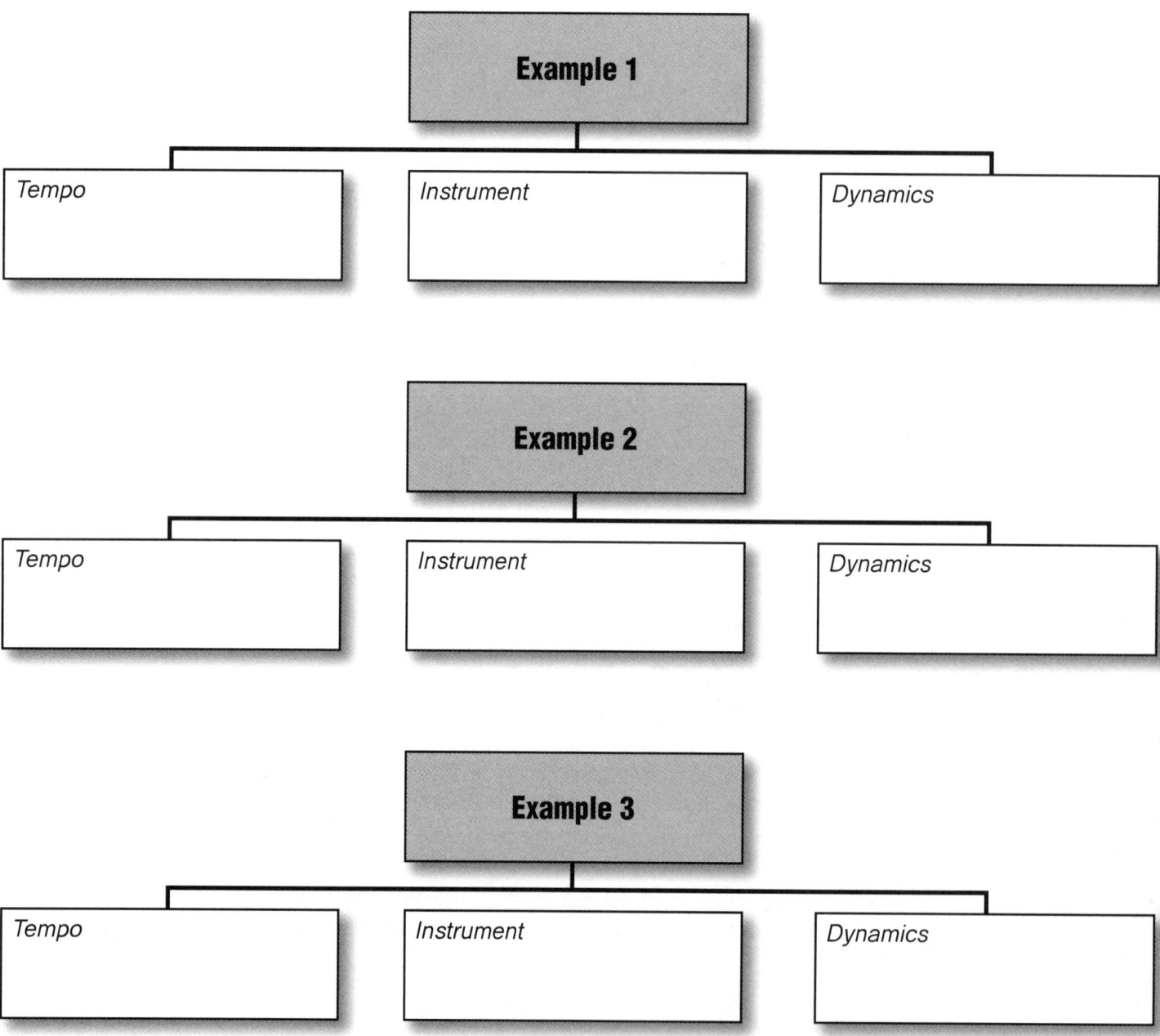

12

From *Music Makes the Scene* by Cathy Blair

Name _____

Date _____

Do You Like to Fly?

As you watch and listen to the three versions of *Do You Like to Fly?*, circle the letter of the word or group of words that best completes the statements (or answers the questions) below.

Example 1

1. What is the tonality of this clip?
   A. Major
   B. Minor

2. This example demonstrates phrase lengths of _____ measures.
   A. 4
   B. 3
   C. 5

3. _____ are two families of instruments heard in this example.
   A. Brass and electronic
   B. String and brass
   C. String and percussion

Example 2

1. This in an example of _____ music, which has its roots in Cuba and New York City.
   A. Tango
   B. Salsa
   C. Bossa nova

2. The repetitive phrase is a (an) _____.
   A. ostinato or montuno
   B. clave or cabasa
   C. sonata or rondo

3. This example uses _____ rhythms.
   A. whole-note
   B. short
   C. syncopated

Example 3

1. What is the time signature of this piece?
   A. It doesn't have one
   B. $\frac{4}{4}$
   C. $\frac{6}{8}$

2. What instruments do you think were used to create most of the sounds in this example?
   A. Guitars
   B. Reeds
   C. Synthesizers

3. Which words best describe the style of this example?
   A. Modern, cinematic
   B. Romantic, legato
   C. Theme and variations, staccato

From *Music Makes the Scene* by Cathy Blair

Name _____

Date _____

Do You Like to Fly?

For discussion: What kind of music do you think would be best suited to go with the short movie you just watched? Should it be fast or slow? Loud or soft? Would electric or acoustic instruments be played? Would the style of music stay the same throughout? What other musical things can you think of that would help bring this video to life?

As you watch each of the three versions with music, write a word or phrase that describes the mood of the music in each clip (happy, bright, scary, etc.) in each of the three ovals below.

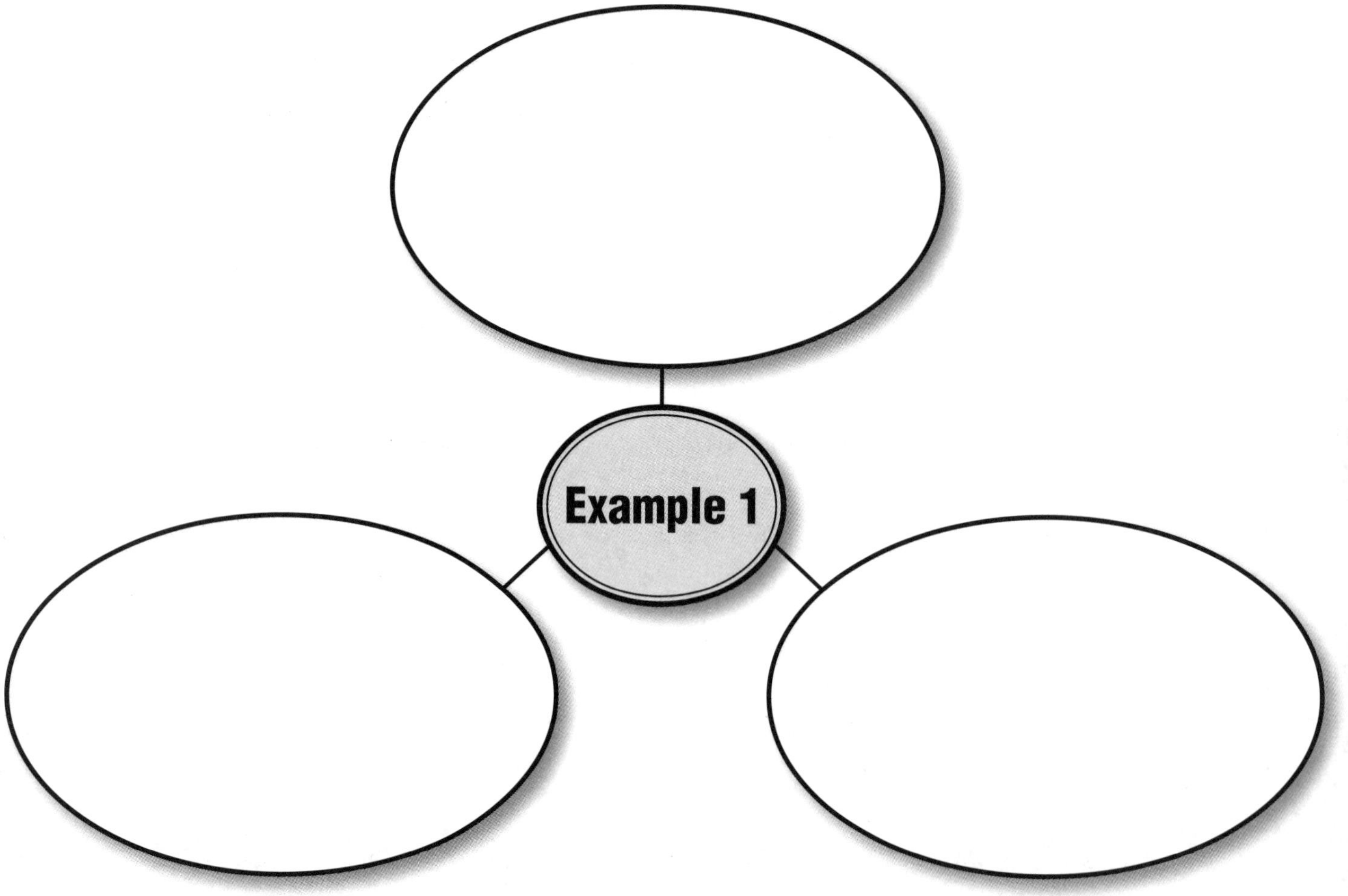

Example 1

From *Music Makes the Scene* by Cathy Blair

Name _____

Date _____

Do You Like to Fly? (page 2)

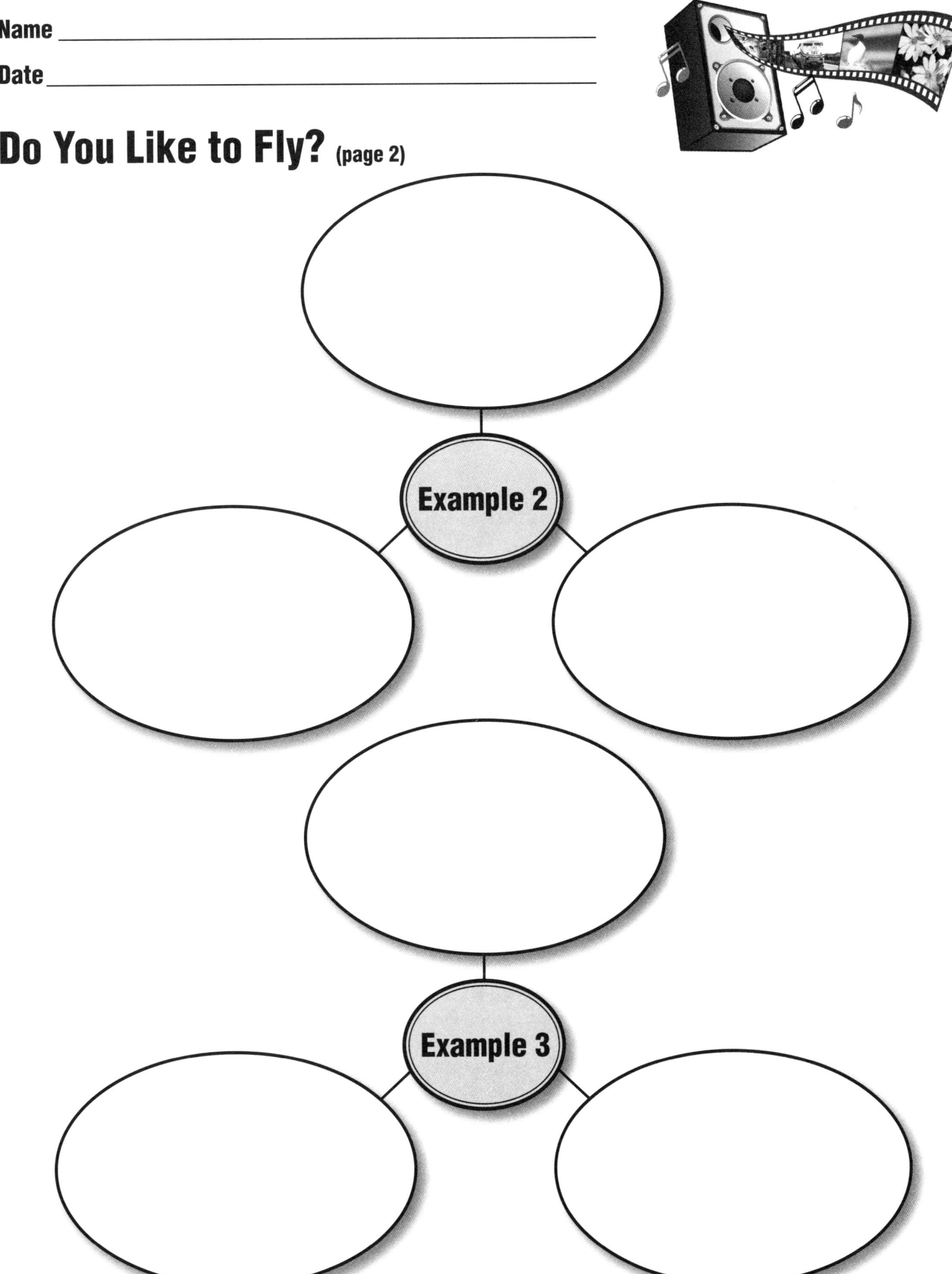

From *Music Makes the Scene* by Cathy Blair

Name _____

Date _____

From the Treetops

As you watch and listen to the three versions of *From the Treetops*, circle the letter of the word or group of words that best completes the following statements.

Example 1

1. _____ is the main solo instrument in this example.
   A. Saxophone   B. Electric guitar   C. Xylophone

2. A _____ is played in this example.
   A. drum set   B. conga drum   C. talking drum

3. Select the group of words that best describes the mood of this example.
   A. Party, rowdy, fun B. Reflective, somber, intimate   C. Soft, soothing, calm

Example 2

1. The first section of this example demonstrates _____.
   A. decrescendo   B. ostinato   C. meter change

2. What is the time signature of this example?
   A. $\frac{2}{4}$ B. There isn't one   C. $\frac{4}{4}$

3. Select the group of words that best describes the mood of this example.
   A. Party, rowdy, fun B. Thoughtful, introspective, soothing   C. Fast, wild, celebration

Example 3

1. The instruments used in this example are _____.
   A. electric   B. acoustic   C. strings

2. Select the list that includes three of the instruments you hear in this example.
   A. Clarinet, tuba, wood block   B. Trombone, violin, guitar   C. Trumpet, trombone, harmonica

3. Select the group of words that best describes the mood of this example.
   A. Thoughtful, sentimental, romantic
   B. Playful, raucous, cartoon-like
   C. Melancholy, slow, introspective

16

From *Music Makes the Scene* by Cathy Blair

Name _____

Date _____

From the Treetops

For discussion: What kind of music would you like to hear with the film clip you just watched? Should it be fast or slow? Loud or soft? Would it use electric or acoustic instruments? Would the style of music stay the same throughout? What other musical things can you think of that would help bring this video to life?

As you watch each of the three versions with music, write an instrument that you hear in each clip in each of the three ovals below.

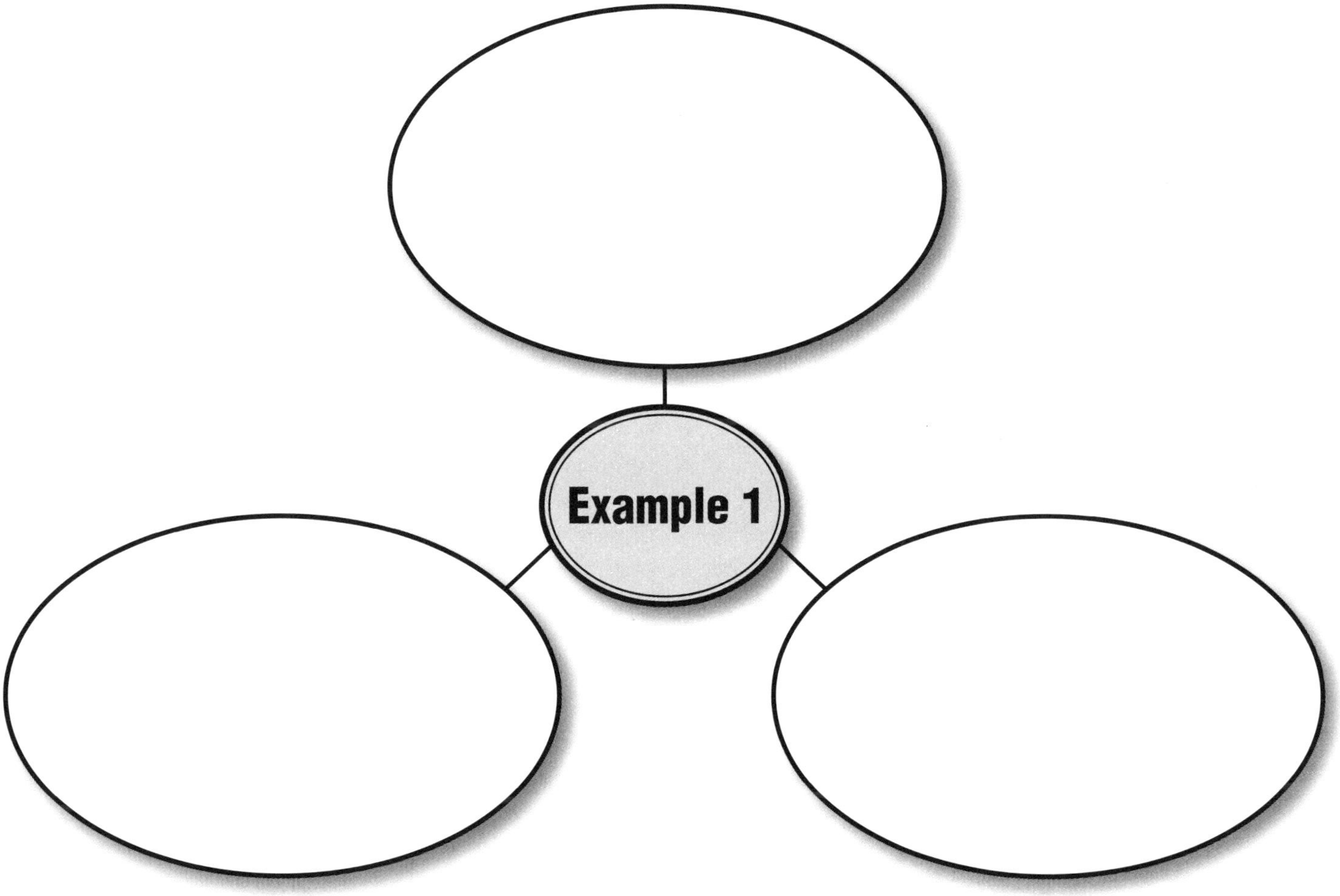

Example 1

Bonus question: Does the music in all three of the clips have a definite tempo?

YES   **NO**

From *Music Makes the Scene* by Cathy Blair

Name _____

Date _____

From the Treetops (page 2)

- Example 2
- Example 3

Name _____

Date _____

Night Vision

As you watch and listen to the three versions of *Night Vision*, circle the letter that best answers the questions (or completes the statements) below.

Example 1
1. Which list includes three of the instruments you hear in this example?
    A. Drum set, electric guitar, electric piano (synthesizer)
    B. Electric guitar, saxophone, conga drums
    C. Trumpet, drum set, xylophone

2. What is the solo instrument that enters midway through this example?
    A. Cello   B. Alto saxophone   C. Harmonica

3. Which group of words best describes this music example?
    A. Urban, cool, contemporary
    B. Salsa, legato, $\frac{3}{4}$ meter
    C. Soothing, orchestral, bossa nova

Example 2
1. There are _____ musicians playing in this example.
    A. 2   B. 4   C. 6

2. This example demonstrates _____.
    A. $\frac{4}{4}$ meter   B. polyphonic music   C. Blues

3. Which group of words best describes this music example?
    A. Laid-back, syncopated, quintet   B. Driving, edgy, rock   C. European, Baroque, elegant

Example 3
1. What kind of ensemble is playing this example?
    A. Brass quintet   C. Concert band   C. Neither

2. Most of the music in this example is _____.
    A. acoustic   B. electric   C. neither

3. The music in this example is _____.
    A. out of tempo   B. in tempo   C. both in and out of tempo

From *Music Makes the Scene* by Cathy Blair

Name _____

Date _____

Night Vision

Briefly describe the music in each of the three film clips. Include specific music terms (tempo, time signature, dynamic range, instrumentation, phrase length, etc.) along with words that describe the mood of the music.

Example 1

_____
_____
_____
_____
_____
_____
_____

Example 2

_____
_____
_____
_____
_____
_____
_____

Example 3

_____
_____
_____
_____
_____
_____
_____

From *Music Makes the Scene* by Cathy Blair

Name _____

Date _____

Mad Rush

As you watch and listen to the three versions of *Mad Rush*, circle the letter of the word or group of words that best completes the following statements.

Example 1

1. Based on its style, _____ is a possible composer of this example.
   A. Hector Berlioz   B. Igor Stravinsky   C. W.A. Mozart

2. _____ best describes the instrumental ensemble performing this example.
   A. String quartet   B. Piano trio   C. Chamber orchestra

3. The music in this example is in a _____ style.
   A. Romantic   B. Classical   C. Baroque

Example 2

1. The two instruments playing the melody in this example are the _____.
   A. saxophone and violin   B. saxophone and trumpet   C. saxophone and guitar

2. Two other instruments heard in this example are the _____.
   A. piano and bass   B. trombone and trumpet   C. drum set and shaker

3. _____ best describes the style of the music in this example.
   A. Techno   B. Jazz   C. Bluegrass

Example 3

1. What is the time signature of this example?
   A. $\frac{4}{4}$ B. $\frac{12}{8}$ C. It doesn't have one.

2. The notes played by the electric bass in this example mainly _____.
   A. stay the same   B. ascend   C. descend

3. _____ is one of the instruments used in this example.
   A. Bassoon   B. Strayhorn   C. Synthesizer

From *Music Makes the Scene* by Cathy Blair   21

Name _____

Date _____

Mad Rush

As you watch each of the three film clips with music, fill in the charts below as directed.

Example 1
Three possible composers of this music

Example 2
Three instruments you hear

Example 3
Three words that describe the mood of this music

From *Music Makes the Scene* by Cathy Blair

Name _____

Date _____

March of the Penguins

As you watch and listen to the three versions of *March of the Penguins*, circle the letter of the word or group of words that best completes the following statements.

Example 1

1. The _____ family of instruments is used throughout this example.
   A. string	B. woodwind	C. percussion

2. You might expect to hear this style of music at a _____.
   A. movie	B. concert	C. basketball game

3. _____ is the one instrument that comes in on the first beat of the first measure and plays continuously to the end of this example.
   A. Piano	B. Shaker	C. Timpani

Example 2

1. This example demonstrates _____.
   A. sonata form	B. text painting	C. mixed meter

2. The three families of instruments heard in this example are _____.
   A. brass, woodwind, string	B. woodwind, percussion, string	C. percussion, woodwind, brass

3. _____ best describes the style of this example.
   A. Cartoon music	B. Opera	C. Zydeco

Example 3

1. This example uses a combination of _____.
   A. acoustic instruments and synthesizer effects
   B. jazz and classical music
   C. theme and variations and free-form music

2. Select the word that best describes the style of this example.
   A. Cinematic	B. Graceful	C. Baroque

3. One possible composer of this example is _____.
   A. Robert Schumann	B. G.F. Handel	C. James Horner

From *Music Makes the Scene* by Cathy Blair

Name _____

Date _____

March of the Penguins

After you watch the film clip with no music, answer the following questions as if you were going to compose its score.

What instruments would you use?

_____

_____

_____

What tempo would you use for your composition? _____

Do you think your composition would be in a major key or a minor key? Why?

_____

_____

_____

What would the overall mood or feeling of your music be?

_____

_____

_____

What kinds of "non-music" sound effects would you add?

_____

_____

_____

Name _____

Date _____

March of the Penguins

As you watch each of the three film clips with music, fill in the charts below as directed.

Example 1
Three percussion instruments you hear

Example 2
Three percussion instruments you hear

Example 3
Three families of instruments you hear

From *Music Makes the Scene* by Cathy Blair

Name _____

Date _____

Ocean's Island

As you watch and listen to the three versions of *Ocean's Island*, circle the letter of the word or group of words that best completes the following statements.

Example 1

1. Select the group of words that best describes the mood of this example.
   A. Light, freewheeling, comical
   B. Happy, carefree, exotic
   C. Mysterious, uncertain, searching

2. You might expect to hear this example _____.
   A. at a movie   B. at an orchestra concert   C. while studying Cuban music

3. The style of this music suggests that it was written in _____.
   A. 1929   B. 1945   C. 1999

Example 2

1. This example uses all _____ instruments.
   A. acoustic   B. electric   C. wind

2. This example uses the _____ time signature.
   A. $\frac{6}{8}$ B. $\frac{4}{4}$ C. Neither

3. Select the group of words that best describes the mood of this music.
   A. Driving, forceful, adventurous
   B. Threatening, menacing, zany
   C. Spacey, heavenly, calming

Example 3

1. The music in this example is in a _____ style.
   A. gospel   B. jazz   C. rock

2. The solo instrument in this example is the _____.
   A. saxophone   B. piano   C. clarinet

3. _____ musicians are playing the music in this example.
   A. Three   B. Five   C. Six

From *Music Makes the Scene* by Cathy Blair

Name _____

Date _____

Ocean's Island

For discussion: What kind of music do you think would be best suited to go with the short movie you just watched? Should it be fast or slow? Loud or soft? Would electric or acoustic instruments be played? Would the style of music stay the same throughout? What other musical things can you think of that would help bring this video to life?

As you watch each of the three film clips with music, write three words in the each of the charts that describe the tempo and rhythmic activity of the music in each example.

Example 1

Example 2

Example 3

From *Music Makes the Scene* by Cathy Blair

Name _____

Date _____

Tales of the Tribesmen

As you watch and listen to the three versions of *Tales of the Tribesmen*, circle the word or group of words that best answers the questions (or completes the statements) below.

Example 1

1. The tempo of the second section of music is _____ the first section.
    A. slower than B. faster than C. the same as

2. Which family of instruments is used in this example?
    A. String B. Woodwind C. Neither

3. Which pair of words best describes the style or mood of this example?
    A. Modern, cinematic B. Orchestral, floating C. Renaissance, opera

Example 2

1. The tempo of the second section of music in this example is _____ the first section.
    A. slower than B. faster than C. the same as

2. Compared to the first section, the second section of this example is _____.
    A. dark and ominous B. light and breezy C. bright and cheery

3. This example uses no _____.
    A. strings B. rhythm C. harmony

Example 3

1. The tempo of the second section of music in this example is _____ the first section.
    A. slower than B. faster than C. the same as

2. The solo in the first section of this example is a _____.
    A. marimba B. female voice C. male voice

3. What is the style of the second section of music in this example?
    A. Jazz B. Rock C. Hip-hop

From *Music Makes the Scene* by Cathy Blair

Name _____

Date _____

Tales of the Tribesmen

As you watch and listen to this film clip, you'll notice that the visuals and accompanying music change midway through, dividing the clip into two, distinct sections. For each example, identify and list two things that are the same about the music in both sections, and three things that are different. After you have completed the list, write the things that are the same in the area where the circles overlap and the things that are different in the sections of the circles that do not overlap. (If you wrote down a quality that is unique to the first section, you may want to write it in the left section of the diagram. Statements that focus on the second section could be written in the right-hand section.)

Example 1

Same: **Different:**

_____   _____

_____   _____

                                                                      _____

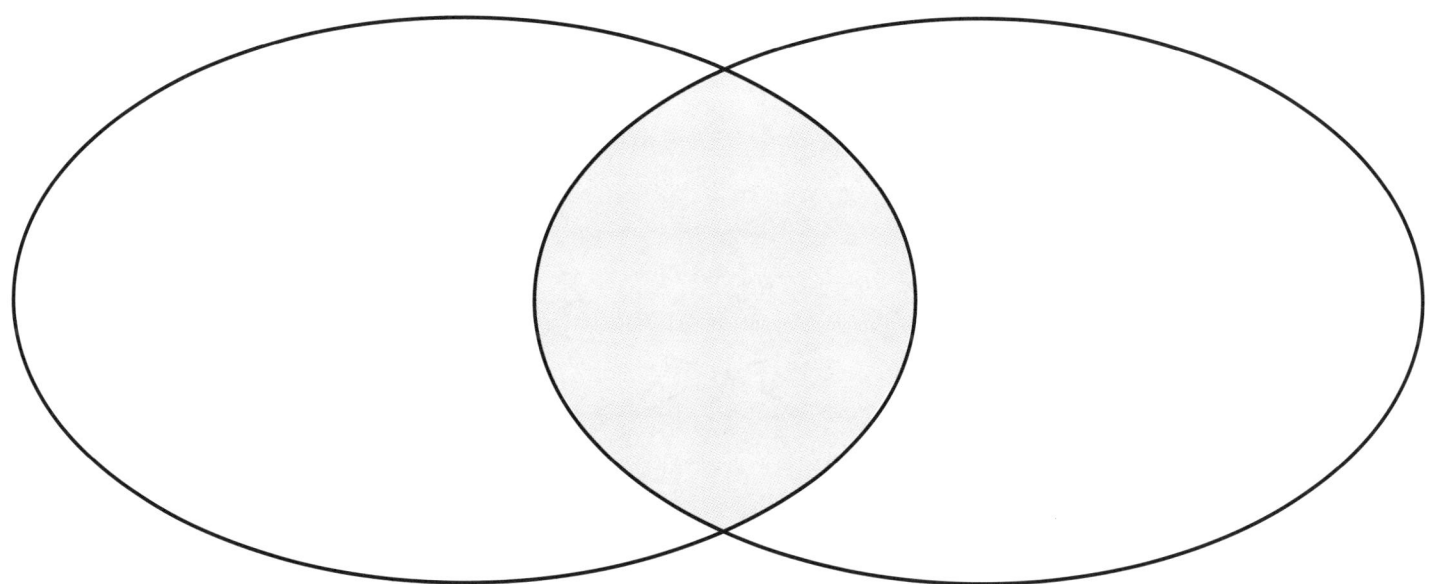

From *Music Makes the Scene* by Cathy Blair

Name _____

Date _____

Tales of the Tribesmen (page 2)

Example 2

Same:

_____

_____

Different:

_____

_____

_____

Example 3

Same:

_____

_____

Different:

_____

_____

_____

From *Music Makes the Scene* by Cathy Blair

Name _____

Date _____

Episode in Space

As you watch and listen to the three versions of *Episode in Space*, circle the letter of the word or group of words that best answers the questions (or completes the statements) below.

Example 1

1. Which list of words best describes the mood of the music in this example?
   A. Uplifting, motivational, driving
   B. Spacey, danger looming, haunting
   C. Joyous, happy, serene

2. Which family of instruments is heard in this example?
   A. Brass   B. Woodwind   C. Neither

3. Who is a possible composer of this music?
   A. Maurice Jarre   B. Ludwig van Beethoven   C. George Gershwin

Example 2

1. The style of this music suggests that it was written in _____.
   A. 1948   B. 1970   C. 2003

2. The music in this example is divided into _____ sections.
   A. two   B. four   C. five

3. Which list of words best describes the music in this example?
   A. Haunting, crisis approaching, scary
   B. Pop/rock rhythm section, fun, light
   C. Chaotic, gritty, hard rock

Example 3

1. What term best describes the end of the music in this example?
   A. ritardando   B. allegro   C. diminuendo

2. The style of this music suggests that it was written in _____.
   A. 1926   B. 1830   C. 1774

3. What are the two instrument families heard in this example?
   A. Woodwind and brass   B. Woodwind and percussion   C. Woodwind and string

From *Music Makes the Scene* by Cathy Blair

Name _____

Date _____

Episode in Space

As you watch each of the three versions with music, write three words or phrases that describe the mood of the music in each clip (happy, bright, scary, etc.) in each of the charts below.

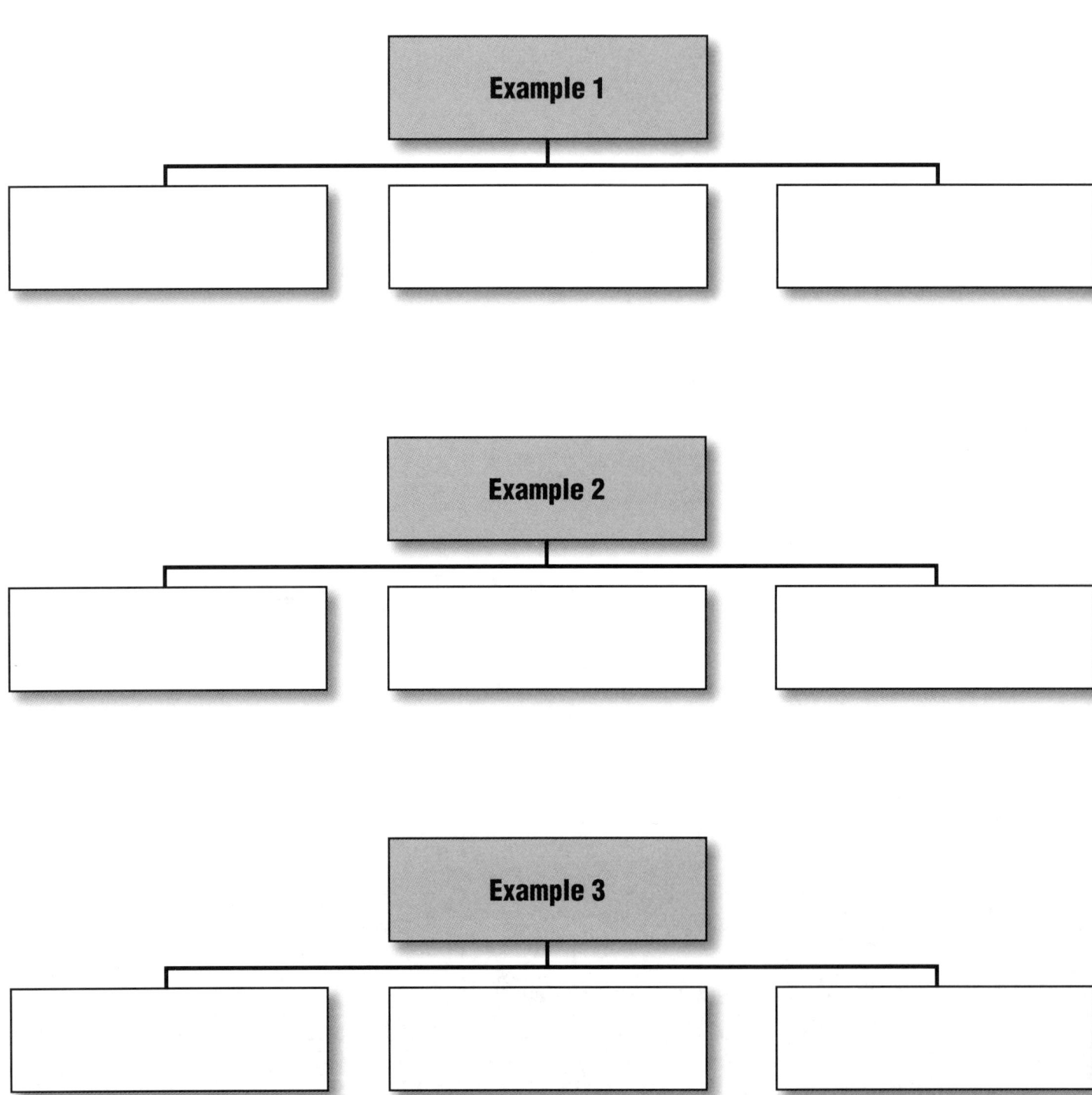

32 From *Music Makes the Scene* by Cathy Blair

Their Music Makes the Scene
Short biographies of several well-known film composers

Danny Elfman

In the 1980s, Danny Elfman was in a pop band called Oingo Boingo. (Really.) But later in that decade, he worked with director Tim Burton on *Beetlejuice, Batman* and *Edward Scissorhands,* which launched his career as a film composer.

Other movies that Danny Elfman wrote music for include:
- *Scrooged*
- *Good Will Hunting*
- *Men In Black*
- *Spiderman 1 and 2*
- *Charlie and the Chocolate Factory*

He also wrote the music for the following TV shows:
- *The Simpsons*
- *Tales from the Crypt*
- *Desperate Housewives*

Randy Newman

Nearly all of Randy Newman's family is involved in writing and producing music for movies. He has been nominated for many awards and won an Oscar for best song in a movie for "If I Didn't Have You" from *Monsters, Inc.*

Other movies with music by Randy Newman include:
- *Parenthood*
- *Toy Story 1 and 2*
- *Maverick*
- *Meet the Parents*
- *A Bug's Life*
- *Cars*

Bill Conti

Bill Conti is recognized for his ability to bridge the gap between various music styles. The best example of this is the music for the *Rocky* movies, which combines classic film composing with elements of rock music. Conti won an Oscar for the music he wrote for the movie *The Right Stuff*. He also served as the music director for the Academy Awards show during the 1990s.

Other movies with music by Bill Conti include:
- *The Karate Kid* (all 3 movies)
- *For Your Eyes Only*
- *Masters of the Universe*
- *Spy Hard*

John Williams

John Williams is almost certainly the most famous film composer in history. He found his first success in Hollywood adapting the music of Jerry Bock in the movie version of *Fiddler on the Roof* (for which he won his first Oscar). Around the same time, a new director named Steven Spielberg came on the scene. He asked John Williams to write the music for the movie *Jaws*. This is perhaps the only time that the essence of a character was perfectly captured with only two notes—the two-note theme of the shark. Williams won his second Oscar for the music in this movie.

Williams and Spielberg have teamed up on many other hit movies over the years, including *Close Encounters of the Third Kind, E.T.,* and the *Indiana Jones* movies. John Williams also formed a friendship with director George Lucas. Lucas had him write the music for all the *Star Wars* movies. Williams earned his third Oscar for the music to the first of the *Star Wars* movies.

Aside from being a film composer, John Williams was also the conductor of the Boston Pops Orchestra, and was commissioned to write music for the Olympics and the unveiling of the rejuvenated Statue of Liberty.

John Williams has a very long list of movie credits, but some other highlights (in addition to those films listed above) include:

- *Presumed Innocent*
- *J.F.K.*
- *Home Alone 1 and 2*
- *Jurassic Park 1 and 2*
- *Hook*
- The *Harry Potter* movies
- *Catch Me If You Can*

He also composed the music for the following TV shows:

- *Lost in Space*
- *Land of the Giants*
- *Gilligan's Island*

Hans Zimmer

Hans Zimmer was born in Germany and, like Danny Elfman, his first involvement in the music business was as a member of a pop/rock band. Zimmer's band in Europe was called The Camera Club. Zimmer soon worked his way up through the ranks of TV composers in the United States. His first well-known TV show was the 1980s hit *Miami Vice*. His first film credits include incidental music for *The Lion King* and *Rain Man*.

He has gone on to have a prolific writing career, having composed music for many movies, including:

- *Twister*
- *As Good as It Gets*
- *Gladiator*
- *The Ring*
- *The Da Vinci Code*
- The *Pirates of the Caribbean* movies

James Horner

James Horner studied music at the Royal College of Music in London before moving to Hollywood to begin his film-music career. His music covers a wide variety of styles ranging from bold orchestral scores (*Star Trek*) to sweet and sentimental music (*Land Before Time*) to Celtic music (*Braveheart*).

Like John Williams, James Horner has written music for many, many movies. Some of the biggest include:
- *Clear and Present Danger*
- *An American Tail 1 and 2*
- *Legends of the Fall*
- *Apollo 13*
- *A Beautiful Mind*
- *How the Grinch Stole Christmas*
- *Radio*
- *Titanic*

Lalo Schifrin

If you know the theme to *Mission: Impossible*, you know the music of Lalo Schifrin. His music is often "jazzy" and incorporates elements of pop and rock too. Many of the movies for which he has written music are action-packed thrillers, like the Clint Eastwood *Dirty Harry* series and Bruce Lee's *Enter the Dragon*. Through his connection with Bruce Lee, Schifrin met Jackie Chan and did the music for the *Rush Hour* movies Chan made with Chris Tucker.

Schifrin composed the music to many earlier classic movies too, including:
- *Cool Hand Luke*
- *Bullitt*
- *Kelly's Heroes*
- *Amityville Horror 1 and 2*

In addition to writing the theme for the *Mission: Impossible* TV show (and later, the *Mission: Impossible* movies), Schifrin also composed the jazzy theme for the TV show *Mannix*.

John Barry

Do any of these movie titles ring a bell?
> *From Russia With Love*
> *Goldfinger*
> *Thunderball*
> *You Only Live Twice*
> *Diamonds Are Forever*
> *A View to a Kill*
> *The Living Daylights*

If you recognized these as James Bond movies, you undoubtedly know the music from these movies, especially the great theme song. Even though the actors portraying James Bond have changed over the years—Sean Connery, Roger Moore, Timothy Dalton, Pierce Brosnan, and Daniel Craig*—the film composer—John Barry—has remained constant. He is also adept at composing music for other kinds of movies too.

Some of his other well-known work includes music for:
> *Born Free*
> *Midnight Cowboy*
> *Jagged Edge*
> *Out of Africa*
> *Dances with Wolves* (for which he won an Oscar)

Maurice Jarre

In the 1960s, the French composer Maurice Jarre wrote landmark scores for two epic movies that would become models for film composers for the next 50 years: *Lawrence of Arabia* and *Doctor Zhivago*. His sweeping and expansive themes permeated these movies and cemented Jarre's place in film-music history.

He has stayed very busy since then, writing music for movie hits including:
> *Great Expectations*
> *The Man Who Would be King* (another epic)
> *Mad Max Beyond Thunderdome*
> *Witness*
> *Fatal Attraction*
> *Gorillas in the Mist*
> *Ghost*

---

*For you hard-core Bond fans, two other actors also played James Bond: George Lazenby in *On Her Majesty's Secret Service* and David Niven in the 1967 version of *Casino Royale*.

Name _____
Date _____

Whose Music Made the Scene?

Match each composer to the movie he scored.

Danny Elfman	*Cars*
Randy Newman	*James Bond* movies
Bill Conti	*Rocky* movies
John Williams	*Men In Black*
Hans Zimmer	*Jaws*
James Horner	*Titanic*
Lalo Schifrin	*Pirates of the Caribbean*
John Barry	*Lawrence of Arabia*
Maurice Jarre	*Mission: Impossible*

From *Music Makes the Scene* by Cathy Blair

Answer Keys

Ancient Egypt

Page 8   Multiple-choice worksheet
         Example 1: C, A, C
         Example 2: B, B, B
         Example 3: C, C, C

Page 9   *Ancient Egypt 1*
            Filled in for students
         Ancient Egypt 2
            Any three: Violin, viola, cello, bass, viola, trumpet, trombone, snare drum
         Ancient Egypt 3
            Organ/synthesizer, drum set, (electric) bass

Page 10 The second part of *Ancient Egypt* asks the students to write three words that describe the music in each example, so there are lots of possibilities!

Crystal Effects

Page 11 Multiple-choice worksheet
            Example 1: B, A, C
            Example 2: C, C, A
            Example 3: A, B, A

Page 12 *Crystal Effects 1*
            Tempo: Adagio, Largo (slow)
            Instrument: Harpsichord
            Dynamics: *mezzo forte* throughout (dynamic level stays the same)
         Crystal Effects 2
            Tempo: Medium
            Instrument (any one of these): synthesizer, timpani, drum set, voice, strings
            Dynamics: *forte* to *mezzo forte* (or *mezzo piano*)
         Crystal Effects 3
            Tempo: Presto, Vivace (fast)
            Instrument (any one of these): trumpet, trombone, piano, electric guitar, electric bass, drum set
            Dynamics: *forte*

Do You Like to Fly?

Page 13 Multiple-choice worksheet
            Example 1: B, A, B
            Example 2: B, A, C
            Example 3: A, C, A

Page 14 These will all be subjective answers.

38

From the Treetops

Page 16 Multiple-choice worksheet
     Example 1: B, A, A
     Example 2: A, B, B
     Example 3: B, A, B

Page 17 *From the Treetops 1*
     Any three: electric guitar, electric bass, drum set, triangle, organ
Page 18 *From the Treetops 2*
     Synth, drums, piano
     From the Treetops 3
     Any three: flute, clarinet, (muted) trumpet, tuba, snare drum, cymbals, xylophone, woodblock
     Bonus—No

Night Vision

Page 19 Multiple-choice worksheet
     Example 1: A, C, A
     Example 2: A, B, C
     Example 3: C, B, C

Page 20 These will all be subjective answers.

Mad Rush

Page 21 Multiple-choice worksheet
     Example 1: C, C, B
     Example 2: A, A, B
     Example 3: C, A, C

Page 22 *Mad Rush 1*
     Mozart, Haydn, Gluck (or other composers from the Classical Period)
     Mad Rush 2
     Any three: (tenor) saxophone, violin, piano, (electric) guitar, bass, drum set
     Mad Rush 3
     These will all be subjective answers.

March of the Penguins

Page 23 Multiple-choice worksheet
     Example 1: C, A, B
     Example 2: C, C, A
     Example 3: A, A, C

Page 24 These will all be subjective answers.
Page 25 *March of the Penguins 1*
     Any three: shaker, bell tree, cymbals, (various) drums
     March of the Penguins 2
     Any three: cymbals, tambourine, xylophone, snare drum, cowbell
     March of the Penguins 3
     Any three: strings, woodwinds, brass, electronic

Ocean's Island

Page 26 Multiple-choice worksheet
  Example 1: C, A, C
  Example 2: B, B, A
  Example 3: B, A, B

Page 27 The answers here will be somewhat subjective, but the basic tempo and rhythmic elements of each of the examples are as follows:
  Ocean's Island 1
    Tempo: Medium
    Rhythmic elements: eighth- (or sixteenth-) note patterns with percussion over sustained notes with guitars and synths
  Ocean's Island 2
    Tempo: Fast
    Rhythmic elements: busy eighth- and sixteenth-note patterns
  Ocean's Island 3
    Tempo: Slow
    Rhythmic elements: lots of space, saxophone solo uses "swing" eighth notes

Tales of the Tribesmen

Page 28 Multiple-choice worksheet
  Example 1: A, C, A
  Example 2: C, A, A
  Example 3: C, B, B

Page 29 The answers here will be somewhat subjective, but some possible answers are as follows:
  Tales of the Tribesmen 1
    Same: Some of the same synth effects are used in both sections of the music. The dynamic level stays the same.
    Different: Tempo, instrumentation, mood
Page 30 *Tales of the Tribesman 2*
    Same: Tempo and time signature
    Different: Instrumentation, mood, dynamic level
  Tales of the Tribesmen 3
    Same: Tempo and time signature
    Different: Mood, dynamic level, instrumentation changes from mainly acoustic to mainly electric

Episode in Space

Page 31 Multiple-choice worksheet
  Example 1: B, C, A
  Example 2: C, A, A
  Example 3: A, C, C

Page 32 These will all be subjective answers.

Whose Music Made the Scene?

Page 37 Danny Elfman—*Men In Black*
  Randy Newman—*Cars*
  Bill Conti—*Rocky* movies
  John Williams—*Jaws*
  Hans Zimmer—*Pirates of the Caribbean*
  James Horner—*Titanic*
  Lalo Schifrin—*Mission: Impossible*
  John Barry—James Bond movies
  Maurice Jarre—*Lawrence of Arabia*